McDONNELL DOUGLAS DC-10

ROBBIE SHAW

LONDON
IAN ALLAN LTD

First published 1991

ISBN 0 7110 1948 7

© Ian Allan Ltd 1991

Published by Ian Allan Ltd, Shepperton, Surrey; and printed by Ian Allan Printing Ltd at their works at Coombelands in Runnymede, England

Previous page:
Aeromexico is one of the two operators of the DC-10-15, flying two of this variant alongside three DC-10-30s. The company was declared bankrupt in 1988 by its owners, the Mexican Government, but eventually operations resumed under the name Aerovias de Mexico, though marketing is still carried out under the well known Aeromexico titles. The Series 30 aircraft are used on services to Madrid and Paris.
McDonnell Douglas

Above:
Air Afrique is an international carrier of a consortium of 10 African countries. All the countries concerned have strong ties with France and consequently the airline's three DC-10-30s are a frequent sight at Charles de Gaulle airport. Note the stylised Gazelle's head and globe on the fin. *McDonnell Douglas*

INTRODUCTION

On 29 August 1970 the first McDonnell Douglas DC-10 made its maiden flight from the company's Long Beach facility, becoming the first wide-bodied trijet to fly, stealing a lead on its rival the Lockheed L1011 TriStar.

The story, however, began back in 1966 when American Airlines issued a request to seven airframe manufacturers outlining its specifications for a transcontinental 'mini jumbo'. The then Douglas Aircraft Company submitted its proposal, the DC-10, albeit slightly larger and powered by three engines rather than the two specified by American. However, the airline eventually concurred, and on 19 February placed an order for 25 DC-10s with options on a further 25, forecasting an eventual requirement of 100 aircraft. By this time Douglas had become a division of the giant McDonnell Douglas Corporation, and was fighting a sales war for orders with the rival TriStar. Both aircraft were of similar design, being wide-bodied and powered by turbofan engines, one under each wing with the third mounted at the base of the tailfin. On the TriStar the third engine was mounted deep into the base of the fin, whilst the DC-10 had the engine in an independent nacelle slightly higher up near the base of the fin.

The first variant to emerge from the Long Beach plant was the DC-10-10 series, powered by General Electric CF6-6D or -6D1 engines each producing 40,000 and 41,000lb thrust respectively. Passenger capacity could be varied from 270 mixed class, up to 380 in an all-economy configuration. In the economy section the fuselage was wide enough to permit nine-abreast seating in a two/five/two split, being reduced to six in a two/two/two split in first class.

From the outset, McDonnell Douglas had envisaged several variants of the DC-10, including a long-range version for intercontinental routes, which was initially known as the DC-10 Series 20 and was developed in response to a request from Northwest Orient. The wingspan was increased by 3m, and fuel capacity increased by an amazing two-thirds. To cope with the extra weight a third main undercarriage bogie was installed in the fuselage centreline between the wing-mounted units. The Northwest machines were powered by Pratt & Whitney JT9D-20 turbofans rated at 49,400lb with water injection, and the first Series 20 aircraft flew on 28 February 1972. Northwest was the only customer for the DC-10-20 aircraft, which were later re-designated DC-10-40 series.

In June 1972 the first DC-10-30 flew, and featured the increased wingspan, fuel capacity and undercarriage bogie as the Series 20. This variant was powered by General Electric turbofans producing up to 51,000lb thrust. The Series 30 also became the most prolific of variants, its intercontinental range of 5,150nm (9,544km) compared to 3,652nm (6,768km) on the Series 10 no doubt being a major factor in the amount of export orders it received.

As previously mentioned, the Series 20 aircraft for Northwest were eventually re-designated Series 40, with Japan Air Lines being the only customer to order the Series 40 with JTD-59A turbofans rated at 53,000lb. The first flight of this model took place on 25 July 1975.

The next variant from the Long Beach production line was the Series 30ER, ER standing for extended range. An additional 5,807l fuel tank was installed in the rear cargo compartment,

Far right:
One of the many US airlines which flourished under deregulation in the 1970s was Air Florida. Although it had an extensive domestic service throughout the eastern US, the company successfully obtained a licence to operate a service from its Miami base to London. The DC-10 was chosen to operate this service and for four years aircraft leased at various times from Trans America and World plied the route, before the company went bankrupt in 1984. N1035F was the first DC-10-30 to be leased by Air Florida.
Peter Asbridge collection

increasing the range by up to 200nm (370km), whilst a larger 12,556l tank was also available. Swissair ordered the first two 30ER versions in 1980, as well as kits to convert a further two aircraft already in service. The first large tank to be installed was on a Finnair aircraft enabling that carrier to operate a direct flight over the North Pole from Helsinki to Tokyo, a distance of 5,966nm (11,056km). To cope with the weight of the extra fuel, more powerful General Electric CF6-50C2B engines producing 54,000lb thrust were used on 30ER variants.

Produced in fewer numbers than any other variant was the Series 15. This version was designed specifically to meet the requirements of Mexicana and Aeromexico for hot and high operations. This aircraft is basically a Series 10 airframe with the more powerful Series 30 engines, hence the out-of-sequence designation. This match of airframe and engines enables those airlines to carry maximum payloads from their Mexico City base which is 7,000ft above sea level. The first flight of this variant took place on 8 January 1981, with deliveries to Mexicana commencing in June that year, although the Mexican airlines were the only customers for the Series 15 — a total of only seven aircraft.

Aside from the passenger versions listed above, the company also produced two freighter variants, the first being the DC-10CF. This is a convertible freighter which can be utilised in all-cargo, all-passenger configurations, or a mixture of both. The first CF was a Series 30 aircraft which first flew on 28 February 1973, with initial deliveries going to Overseas National and Trans International. The CF was, however, available in any basic series and Continental took some Series 10CF aircraft. The final type to be developed was the pure freighter DC-10F — like the CF it can carry palletised loads — and the first of this variant was delivered to Federal Express on 24 January 1986. Federal Express ordered nine of this variant which has the capability to carry a 80,282kg (176,992lb) payload over intercontinental distances.

One other vitally important version not yet mentioned is the KC-10A Extender, 60 of which were delivered to the USAF's Strategic Air Command to equip three Wings. Developed in response to a USAF requirement for an advanced tanker/cargo aircraft (ATCA), the DC-10 was announced the winner on 19 December 1977, in preference to the Boeing 747. The KC-10 force greatly enhances the flexibility of the USAF as the aircraft can carry the supporting ground equipment, spares and groundcrews for the combat aircraft it refuels on deployments. The Extender is based on the airframe of the DC-10-30CF, but with a number of additional modifications for its military role. These include additional fuel cells in the lower fuselage, an improved cargo handling facility, and a refuelling receptacle above the cockpit to enable it to be refuelled by other tankers. From the boom operator's station in the lower rear fuselage, the 'boomer' controls the flying boom necessary to refuel other USAF aircraft, and the single hose-and-drogue required for refuelling Navy, Marine Corps and some NATO aircraft. The aerial refuelling boom is more advanced than that used in the Boeing KC-135, in particular the fuel flow rate is faster at 5,678l (1,500US gal)/min.

Since that initial order from American Airlines for 25 aircraft, McDonnell Douglas fought a sales war with the product of its arch rival, the L1011 TriStar. The euphoria at winning the order from American did not last long, as within weeks the TriStar had clocked up no fewer than 168 orders, whilst the DC-10 stagnated at just 25. A sense of gloom hung over the Long Beach plant until United Airlines, which found it difficult to choose between the two types, eventually ordered 60 aircraft, a decision which almost certainly saved the DC-10 programme. With the planned Series 30 variant, a number of export orders started coming in and by the time the prototype took to the air over 200 orders had been received. A number of these were from the KSSU group, which consisted of KLM, Swissair, SAS and UTA. The final DC-10 was delivered in February 1989 to Nigeria Airways, this being the 446th DC-10 built — including 60 KC-10s for the USAF. It is likely that the manufacturers had expected to build more DC-10s than they did; however it must be remembered that the oil crisis is sure to have played a major part in keeping the figures down, and to exacerbate the situation further still there was a general recession on US domestic routes in the mid-1970s. To put it into perspective, production of the competing TriStar ceased in 1983, with only 250 aircraft built.

McDonnell Douglas' successor to the DC-10 is the MD-11, details of which were first released at the 1985 Paris Air Show, with the programme receiving the go-ahead late the following year. The MD-11 is almost identical to its predecessor, with the addition of winglets to reduce drag. Two fuselage lengths are available, one the same length as the DC-10, the other 18.6ft (5.66m) longer. Building on the success of the DC-10 design, passenger, combi and freighter versions will be available, as will

Far right:
The international airline of Fiji, Air Pacific, currently operates a Boeing 747 on routes to Bali, Honolulu and Los Angeles; prior to delivery of the 747 the airline operated a DC-10 on lease. That aircraft also wore the company's striking livery as illustrated here, taxying for departure at Honolulu.
Peter Asbridge collection

an extended range variant. The MD-11 made its maiden flight on 10 January 1990 from Long Beach and a total of four pre-production aircraft will be involved in the flight test programme. A fifth MD-11 will be flown for certification of the Pratt & Whitney PW4460 powerplants. Other engines on offer are the General Electric CF6-80C2 and Rolls-Royce Trent 650, with FAA certification of the aircraft expected in the fall of 1990.

Airlines which have operated the DC-10 over the years are as follows: (those in brackets either no longer operate the type or, indeed, no longer exist).

Aeromaritime, Aeromexico, (Aero Americana), Air Afrique, (Air Algerie*), (Air America), (Air Florida*), (Air Hawaii), (Air New Zealand), (Air Pacific*), (Air Panama*), (Air Seychelles*), (Air Siam), Air Zaire, (Alitalia), (Aloha). American, (American Trans Air), (Ariana), (Arrow Air), Balair, Bangladesh Biman, (Bogazici Hava Tasimaciligi), British Airways, (British Caledonian), (British Midland*), (Cal-Air), Canadian Airlines International, (Canadian Pacific), (Capitol), (Caribbean), Condor, Continental, (Delta), (Dominicana*), Eastern, Ecuatoriana, (Egyptair*), Federal Express, Finnair, Garuda, Ghana Airways, Iberia, (Icelandair*), Japan Air Lines, Japan Air System, Japan Asia, (Jet 24), Jugoslovenski Aerotransport, Key Airlines, KLM, Korean Air, (Laker), (Lan Chile), (Lauda Air*), Lineas Aereas de Mocambique, Lufthansa, Malaysian, Martinair, Mexicana, Minerve, Nationair, (National), Nigeria Airways, Northwest (Orient), Novair, (Overseas National), (Pacific East Air), (Pakistan International Airways), (Pan American), Philippine Airlines, (Point Air*), Sabena, Scanair, SAS, (Singapore Airlines), (Spantax), Sun Country Airlines, Swissair, (TAAG Angola*), Thai International, (The Hawaii Express), (TOA Domestic), (Trans America), (Trans International), (Turk Hava Yollari), Turkish Air, United, UTA, (United Air Carriers International), Varig, Viasa, (Wardair), (Western), World Airways, Zambia Airways.

Operated on lease

I should like to thank a number of friends for their assistance in the preparation and research for this book, including Peter Asbridge, Maurice Bertrand, Ian Logan, Duncan MacIntosh, Leo Marriott, Colin Wood and Paul Wright. Also many thanks to McDonnell Douglas Media Relations Department, Liz Ross at British Airways, KLM, Lufthansa, Mexicana, Scanair, SAS, Singapore Airlines and Varig.

Right:
DC-10 N905WA is photographed here at Long Beach in the colourful markings of Air Hawaii.
Peter Asbridge collection

Left:
Swiss charter operator Balair uses a DC-10-30 for long-haul services to the Caribbean, North and Central America and the Far East. The aircraft, HB-IHK, was photographed landing at Geneva. *Ralf Braun*

The flagship of the Air Zaire fleet is a single DC-10-30 which is a frequent sight at Brussels, with Paris and Rome the only other destinations served outside Africa. The airline was an early customer for the DC-10, and at one time had two of the type in service. Illustrated is 9Q-CLI which was delivered in 1973. *McDonnell Douglas*

One of the world's largest carriers, American Airlines, was the launch customer for the DC-10. The first DC-10 commercial service was undertaken by an American aircraft on 5 August 1971 on the Los Angeles-Chicago route. The company operates both the Series 10 and 30 variants and, apart from the USAF, operates the largest DC-10 fleet, with 58 aircraft in its inventory at the time of writing. Given the name 'Luxury Liner', American DC-10s operate services to a number of European destinations, including London Gatwick and Manchester Ringway. Pictured climbing out of Gatwick is Series 30 N137AA.
Robbie Shaw

Right:
Ariana Afghan Airlines joined the DC-10 club in late 1979 with the delivery of Series 30 YA-LAS. The type was used to serve European destinations until 1985, when it was sold to British Caledonian in favour of two Tupolev Tu-154s. Since that time services to Western Europe have been discontinued.

Right:
Miami-based Arrow Air operated two DC-10-10s on worldwide charters for a couple of years until it ceased passenger services in 1986 due to financial problems. The airline now operates freight only flights using DC-8s.
Peter Asbridge collection

From its Dhaka base, Bangladesh Biman uses four DC-10-30s on its
international routes previously operated by the Boeing 707. Three
ex-Singapore Airlines aircraft joined the fleet in 1983, with a fourth being
added more recently. The first aircraft to join the airline, S2-ACO, was
photographed on approach to London's Heathrow airport.
Robbie Shaw

One of the latest airlines to operate the DC-10 is British Airways. Following the takeover of British Caledonian, BA incorporated the eight Series 30 aircraft it inherited into its own route structure. These aircraft are all based and operated from Gatwick, primarily on routes to the USA, and also some services to Africa and the Middle East. The airline uses the DC-10 in a mixed configuration of first/club/economy class seating, giving a capacity of 218 passengers. The DC-10s in the British Airways fleet are named after well known British forests.

G-BEBL is allocated the name *Forest of Dean*; however, when this photograph was taken the aircraft had recently emerged from the paint shop and had yet to have the name applied to its nose. *Robbie Shaw*

After a government review of civil aviation in 1976, a certain amount of route shuffling occurred between British Airways and Britain's largest independent carrier, British Caledonian. As a result of this, British Caledonian — or B.Cal as it was frequently abbreviated to — was given the routes to South America and Central and West Africa. The DC-10-30 was the aircraft chosen to operate these routes, and two were ordered for delivery the following year. Eventually eight brand new DC-10-30s were taken on charge, also serving B.Cal routes to Hong Kong and the USA, where the Texan destinations of Dallas and Houston were becoming very profitable. The year 1982 proved to be significant for the company: due to the Falklands War, services to South America had to be terminated and this proved a major blow. On the positive side — for

B.Cal that is — the demise of Laker Airways meant increased business for British Caledonian Air Charter, a subsidiary formed to operate tourist charter flights using the former Laker aircraft. This part of the company was later renamed Cal-Air. In 1985 two secondhand aircraft were added to the fleet, though two years later two were sold to Continental Airlines. After a period of financial problems, British Caledonian was taken over in 1988 by one of its strongest competitors, British Airways — a sad end to the largest, and one of the oldest of Britain's independent airlines. No longer would DC-10s and BAC One-Elevens with a 'lion rampant' and distinctive Scottish names be seen around the skies of Gatwick. Four B.Cal DC-10s and one belonging to Wardair are pictured on the stands at Gatwick. *Robbie Shaw*

Right:
Cal-Air, a subsidiary of B.Cal, was originally named British Caledonian Air Charter, and commenced services in 1983 using two ex-Laker DC-10-10s on inclusive tour charters. Initially these were on European routes, but gradually a greater emphasis was placed on transatlantic charters and a third aircraft was added to the fleet in 1986. After the British Airways takeover of B.Cal in 1988 the company became a wholly-owned subsidiary of the Rank Organisation, and the same year was renamed Novair. Photographed at Heraklion is ex-Laker DC-10 G-BJZE.
Leo Marriott

Canadian Airlines International was the name adopted from the merger of two of Canada's largest independent carriers: Canadian Pacific and Pacific Western. An extensive network of domestic and intercontinental destinations is served, the latter using the DC-10s inherited from Canadian Pacific, and Boeing 767s. The company arrowhead logo is included in place of the second last letter of the title, CANADI>N, thereby avoiding the issue of whether to use the English or French spelling. The attractive new livery was first seen in late 1987, when DC-10-30 C-GCPE was photographed on approach to Kai Tak's runway 13. *Robbie Shaw*

Right:

Canadian Pacific, one of the largest airlines in Canada, concentrated on intercontinental services across the Pacific, and the only European destination served by the bright orange DC-10s was Amsterdam. The airline operated eight Series 30 aircraft before coming to an agreement with fellow DC-10 operator United Airlines, when three Series 30 aircraft were exchanged for three Series 10s. A further four Series 30 aircraft were taken on charge in 1986 and the airline's four Boeing 747s were disposed of. The following year, after amalgamation with Pacific Western, Canadian Airlines International was formed. DC-10-30ER C-GCPI *Empress of Auckland,* **in Canadian Pacific's distinctive colour scheme, was photographed at Hong Kong's Kai Tak airport.** *Robbie Shaw*

Left:
The wholly-owned subsidiary of Lufthansa, Condor Flugdienst, uses three DC-10-30 aircraft for long-haul charter flights to European, Far East and American destinations. Illustrated is D-ADSO being pushed back from its stand at Frankfurt-Main. *Robbie Shaw*

Left:
An early customer for the DC-10 was Continental Airlines, which currently uses seven Series 10 aircraft on internal US services. For international services, including Gatwick, eight longer range Series 30 aircraft complement the airline's Boeing 747s. N68048 is a Series 10 aircraft with the title *Employee Owner Ship 1* on the nose, and was photographed at Honolulu. *Robbie Shaw*

Delta Airlines has been one of the strongest supporters of Lockheed's rival to the DC-10, the TriStar, and it currently operates 37 of the type. However, the airline has operated DC-10s on two occasions. Rather ironically, Delta placed an order for five Series 10s in 1971, despite having 25 TriStars on order, as insurance in case of any problems with the Tristar programme. These aircraft were eventually sold to United prior to delivery. However, they were immediately taken on lease until sufficient TriStars had been delivered, and after a few years in service were returned to United. In 1987 Delta took over Western Airlines and its small fleet of DC-10s. These aircraft were subsequently disposed of and Delta now uses only the TriStar on its intercontinental services. Ex-Western DC-10-10 N915WA was photographed at San Diego shortly after the takeover in 1987. *Maurice Bertrand*

Left:
One of the most colourful liveries today is that of Ecuatoriana, the national airline of Ecuador. For long-haul services a DC-10-30 is operated serving some South and North American destinations. The aircraft was bought from Swissair in 1983, and was photographed on approach to Zürich for maintenance by its previous owner. *Ralf Braun*

Left:
Although an established TriStar operator, Eastern Airlines acquired three Series 30 DC-10s to operate the transatlantic service from its Miami base to Gatwick. Services commenced in 1985 although the carrier terminated the service after only 15 months due to heavy losses. One aircraft was sold quickly, and at the time of writing the remaining two are still on the airline's inventory. DC-10-30 N391EA is pictured at Miami in February 1987.
Maurice Bertrand

Below:

The recent takeover of Flying Tigers has made Federal Express the world's largest freight carrier and from its Memphis base the company operates a large fleet of Boeing 747 and DC-10 aircraft on an extensive network of domestic and international routes. Initially a number of secondhand Series 10 combi versions and longer-range Series 30 machines were bought, and subsequently a batch of new-build DC-10-30F variants. The latter were amongst the last DC-10s built. Federal Express currently operates a total of 24 DC-10s. Pictured banking to turn finals at Kai Tak is DC-10-30F N309FE. *Robbie Shaw*

Right:

Garuda Indonesia dropped the 'Airways' from its title to coincide with a new livery introduced in late 1985. One of the largest airlines in South East Asia, Garuda uses six DC-10-30s alongside A300 Airbus aircraft on international services throughout the continent. The introduction of the new colour scheme also coincided with the first-ever Indonesian Air Show, for which it was, quite naturally, the official carrier. The attractive new scheme consists of a white fuselage, with a dark blue fin, in which is a stylised Garuda bird in various shades of blue and turquoise. Commencing its take-off run at Kai Tak for a flight to Jakarta is Series 30, PK-GIF. *Robbie Shaw*

Left:
One of only two customers to operate the Series 40, Japan Air Lines ordered 20 of this variant. The type is used primarily on high density domestic services, but some regional Asian destinations — such as Bangkok, Hong Kong and Singapore — are served by the company's DC-10 fleet. A small number of aircraft have been transferred to its subsidiary, Japan Asia.

DC-10-40 JA8541 was photographed at Hong Kong's Kai Tak airport during a quick turn-round on a Bangkok-Tokyo service. *Robbie Shaw*

Right:

Displaying what is arguably one of the most attractive colour schemes to be seen on a DC-10 is Ghana Airways' Series 30 aircraft, 9G-ANA. The DC-10 is the prestige aircraft of the airline's small fleet, and is used on services to Düsseldorf, London and Rome. Being under-utilised, the aircraft frequently flies services for other carriers. It was photographed at Gatwick whilst operating the London-Entebbe service on behalf of Uganda Airways.
Colin Wood

Below right:

Iberia uses eight Series 30 aircraft for long-range services to the Americas and the Middle East. The airline received its first aircraft, EC-CBN in 1973, only to crash in December that year on final approach to Boston's Logan International airport. Amazingly there were no fatalities amongst either the passengers or crew, but the loss of the first DC-10 had been registered.

Iberia occasionally uses its DC-10s on some short sectors when high load factors demand it — including flights to Heathrow — where EC-CSK *Cornisa Cantabrica* was photographed on approach.
Robbie Shaw

Formerly known as Toa Domestic Airlines, Japan Air System was the name chosen when the carrier was permitted to operate international services. To complement its fleet of Airbus A300s, two DC-10-30ER have been purchased and operate services to Singapore and Seoul. *A. Okuda*

Far left:
Formed in 1975, Japan Asia is a wholly-owned subsidiary of Japan Air Lines and operates a few Boeing 747s and DC-10-40s given by the parent company. The airline was formed to operate services from Japan to Taiwan which, for political reasons, its parent company does not. A daily service is operated to Kaohsiung and Taipei via Hong Kong, where JA8532 was photographed.
Robbie Shaw

Left:
Formed in 1979 to operate worldwide passenger and cargo charter services, Jet 24 ceased operations in 1988. Types operated included the Boeing 707, 747 and DC-10. Of the latter, Series 40 N144JC is illustrated.
Peter Asbridge collection

Below left:
Using DC-10-30s, Jugoslovenski Aerotransport (JAT) serves North America, the Middle East and even Australia. More recently Beijing was added to the airline's route structure. At times an additional aircraft has been leased from Air Afrique and Finnair to cope with demand. Photographed prior to delivery is YU-AMA, the first of the type to be delivered to the company. *McDonnell Douglas*

A recent acquisition by Key Airlines is a DC-10-10 N917JW. The aircraft has joined eight Boeing 727s which provide ad-hoc and contract passenger services throughout the USA, where one of the main customers is the US Department of Defense. *Peter Asbridge collection*

An early customer for the Series 30 aircraft was KLM Royal Dutch Airlines. The airline received 11 aircraft for use on some North American routes, although they were primarily intended to serve Far East destinations. Over the years a number were leased out to other airlines, principally Garuda and Viasa. Six aircraft have since been disposed of and now Boeing 747s operate most of the intercontinental routes. Photographed on its landing roll at Amsterdam's Schipol airport is PH-DTD. *Ralf Braun*

Right:
Korean Air took delivery of three new DC-10-30s in 1975, with a further two secondhand machines joining the fleet a few years later. The type is used mainly on international services within Asia, although Libya, Hawaii and the Middle East feature in the schedules. One of the secondhand aircraft was used mainly as a freighter, and this aircraft was written-off in a crash at Anchorage in 1983 when, in thick fog, the aircraft took-off on the wrong runway and collided with a light aircraft. Amazingly there were no fatalities on either aircraft. The airline lost another DC-10 in July 1989, again in foggy weather, this time crashing short of the runway at Tripoli, Libya, but on this occasion there were fatalities. A contributory cause, perhaps, was the fact that the Instrument Landing System (ILS) apparently was not functioning.

In 1984 Korean Air adopted a new pale blue livery and company motif — the 'Taeguk' from the national flag. Displaying the new scheme at Kai Tak is HL7328, the aircraft which crashed at Tripoli.
Robbie Shaw

Lan-Chile ordered two DC-10-30s in 1981, and the aircraft were delivered the following year for use on its European schedules to Frankfurt, Madrid and Rome, and US destinations including Miami and New York. These routes were previously operated by ageing Boeing 707s. In 1986 however, Lan-Chile took delivery of two Boeing 767ERs for its intercontinental services and, after only four years' service, its DC-10s were sold. Photographed at Miami is CC-CJS. *Peter Asbridge collection*

Above:
Linhas Aereas de Mocambique (LAM) is the national carrier of this former Portuguese colony, and was formed as long ago as 1936. It was originally named Direcao de Exploracao dos Transportes Aeroes (DETA), and was given its present title in 1980. A DC-10 Series 30 acquired in 1982 operates services outside the African continent to East Berlin, Copenhagen, Lisbon, Madrid and Paris. The airline's sole DC-10 (illustrated) is French-registered F-GDJK and is named after the country's capital Maputo. *Peter Asbridge collection*

Right:
Only a couple of weeks before the maiden flight of the DC-10, Deutsche Lufthansa ordered five Series 30 aircraft to be used on the airline's routes to the Americas and the Far East. Further examples were ordered, and by 1976 the company had a fleet of 11 McDonnell Douglas trijets. Lufthansa still operates 11 DC-10s whilst its subsidiary, Condor Flugdienst, operates a further three.

Being pushed back from its stand at Frankfurt is D-ADGO. In the background is one Condor, and a further two company DC-10s, one of which is in the new livery adopted in 1989 which incorporates an all-white fuselage. *Robbie Shaw*

Malaysian Airlines System (MAS) was formed in 1971 after the Malaysia-Singapore Airlines consortium ended. A further name change to Malaysia Airlines occurred in 1987, coinciding with an attractive new livery which retains the distinctive Malaysian Kalantan Kite motif on the fin. A trio of DC-10-30s, the first of which was delivered in 1976, operate to Asian destinations but also supplement the Boeing 747 on some services to Australia, Europe and the USA. Flaring for touchdown on runway 13 at Kai Tak is 9M-MAT. Malaysian uses both Airbus A300s and DC-10s on its Kuala Lumpur-Hong Kong services. *Robbie Shaw*

Dutch charter operator Martinair took delivery of its first Series 30CF combi aircraft in 1973, and by the end of the decade had a fleet of four. From its headquarters at Amsterdam's Schipol airport the company operates both cargo and passenger services to a variety of destinations worldwide. The airline recently commenced scheduled passenger services to the USA, and currently operates three DC-10s.

PH-MBP carries the name *Hong Kong* on the nose, and appropriately was photographed departing that airfield. *Robbie Shaw*

Mexicana was formed in 1921, and claims to be the fourth oldest airline in the world. Operating from Mexico City, which has an altitude of 7,000ft, the airline uses five DC-10-15 for services within Latin America and to the USA. Designed for 'hot and high' operations Mexicana use the DC-10 in a single-class configuration of 315 seats. Three aircraft were delivered in 1981 with another two following in 1983. Photographed prior to delivery this aircraft is named *Azteca*. *McDonnell Douglas*

Formed in 1934, National Airlines ordered DC-10-10s for use on internal US services from its Miami base. On receiving licences to operate to a number of European capitals, the airline ordered four longer range Series 30 aircraft before the company was taken over by Pan-American in January 1980. The sixth DC-10-10 to be delivered was N65NA, which is illustrated. *Peter Asbridge collection*

A single DC-10 is a recent acquisition by French charter operator Minerve. Operating from Paris Orly and Nimes-Garons, the airline flies charter and inclusive-tour flights to destinations worldwide. The DC-10, F-GGMZ, is used on services to French colonies in the West Indies and Pacific. *Peter Asbridge collection*

Right:
Gatwick-based Novair International Airways, known as Cal-Air until 1988, uses Boeing 737s and DC-10s on charters to the Mediterranean and North America. The name change followed the sale of the British Airways shareholding and the company is now a wholly-owned subsidiary of the Rank Organisation. The same three ex-Cal-Air DC-10-10s are still used, two of which are ex-Laker Airways machines. The airline livery is still based on the Cal-Air scheme of a broad red band running the length of the fuselage, only the tail insignia differing, a star motif replacing the lion rampant. Photographed on approach to Gatwick is G-BJZE (former Laker aircraft, G-GSKY). *Robbie Shaw*

Below right:
Receiving the first of two DC-10-30s in 1976, Nigeria Airways used the type to replace Boeing 707s on services to New York. Subsequently the European destinations of Amsterdam, London and Rome were frequented by the DC-10s. The type also has been utilised on Haj flights for the annual pilgrimage to Mecca. One aircraft was lost in a crew training accident in January 1987. The airline has the distinction of operating the last DC-10 to leave the McDonnell Douglas production line, which was delivered early in 1989 and that aircraft is illustrated here during a turn round at Heathrow. *Robbie Shaw*

Formed in 1934, Northwest Airlines – formerly known as Northwest Orient – operates 20 DC-10-40s on services to a number of transpacific destinations. However, more recently – with a number of transatlantic gateways being served – the 'Orient' part of the title was omitted. European points in the company network include Dublin and Shannon in Ireland, Gatwick and Prestwick in the UK, Frankfurt in West Germany, plus the Scandinavian capital cities of Copenhagen, Oslo and Stockholm. Both DC-10s and Boeing 747s are used on most of these routes with Series 40 N162US photographed on approach to Honolulu.
Robbie Shaw

Left:
A DC-10 operator since 1974 when it leased two examples from KLM, Philippine Airlines received two Series 30 aircraft of its own two years later. The type was initially used on US services until the introduction of the Boeing 747. The DC-10s are currently used on routes to Australia and Bangkok, and to supplement the Airbus A300 on regional routes when load factors demand. The airline's livery used to consist of a red/blue cheatline and tail markings in the colours of the national flag. An attractive new scheme was introduced in 1987 and the fin marking was revised by adding a yellow rising sun superimposed on the blue, whilst the fuselage adopted an all-white scheme. Displaying the attractive new livery at Bangkok's Don Muang airport is RP-C2003. *Robbie Shaw*

Above:
SABENA Belgian World Airlines uses five DC-10-30CFs for intercontinental services to North America and Africa. The first DC-10, OO-SLA, was delivered to Brussels in 1973, the last in 1980.
McDonnell Douglas

Scanair is a Stockholm-based Scandinavian subsidiary of SAS, and operates inclusive-tour and charter flights to many Mediterranean and North African holiday resorts, as well as the Canary Islands. Until recently the company operated a fleet of ex-SAS Douglas DC-8-63s; however, these have been sold and replaced by six DC-10-10s which are becoming a frequent sight at Stansted, bringing Scandinavian tourists to the UK on shopping expeditions. A longer-range DC-10-30 was operated on lease from SAS briefly in 1986-87. Illustrated is Scanair's first DC-10, SE-DHT. Note the similarity of the colour scheme to that of the parent company. *Scanair*

SAS Scandinavian Airlines System is a member of KSSU (the initials are derived from the first letter of each member: KLM, SAS, Swissair and UTA), the European consortium which ordered a number of Series 30 aircraft. Two aircraft were ordered initially, followed by another three, and the type entered service on the transpolar route to Tokyo in late 1974. Unlike many other airlines, where the DC-10 was replaced on intercontinental routes by the Boeing 747, the reverse is true with SAS. The airline found that its load factors on most routes made the use of Jumbos uneconomic, and the 747 was dispensed with in favour of more DC-10s. Over the years the airline has increased its DC-10 fleet, and currently has 10 aircraft in its inventory. Photographed landing at Chicago O'Hare is OY-KDB *Frode Viking*.   Duncan MacIntosh

A confirmed Boeing operator, Singapore Airlines surprised many people
when it ordered four Series 30 DC-10s, with options on a further four.
Deliveries commenced in mid-1978, and the type replaced some
Boeing 707s which were still in use on regional Asian services. As it
happens, only seven aircraft were taken on strength, and all were sold
off by the end of 1983. This graceful air-to-air study features Singapore's
first DC-10, 9V-SDA. *Singapore Airlines*

Based at Minneapolis-St Paul, Sun Country Airlines was formed in 1982 by a group of ex-Braniff employees. Using a couple of Boeing 727s, the company operates holiday charters to US destinations. In 1986 a DC10-40 – N144JC – formerly used by Jet 24 was acquired, and is used on services to Mexico and the Caribbean. It is pictured here on approach to Las Vegas. *Maurice Bertrand*

Right:
Swissair – a member of the KSSU group which also comprises KLM, SAS and UTA – was first to operate a commercial service with the Series 30. Ultimately the airline received 13 DC-10s, which served on the airline's intercontinental routes worldwide although the fleet has since shrunk to 10, four of which are Series 30ER aircraft. The airline will be one of the first to receive the MD-11. The undercarriage is still retracting as HB-IHI *Fribourg* makes a steep climb-out from Toronto.
Robbie Shaw

Far right:
One of the most attractive airline colour schemes is that applied to Thai International aircraft. Formed in 1959 with the assistance of SAS, the airline leased two DC-10-30s in 1975 until its own aircraft were delivered in 1977. These undertook services to Australia, Europe and the USA, until relieved on most of these routes by the Boeing 747 in the early 1980s. For the next few years the aircraft were under utilised, sometimes supplementing Airbus A300s on regional Asian routes. The two aircraft were eventually sold after three Series 30ER variants entered service in early 1988. Series 30 HS-TGE named *Hariphunchai* has been sold since this photograph was taken of it landing at Kai Tak in December 1986. *Robbie Shaw*

Right:
United Airlines is the second largest commercial DC-10 operator. With a fleet that currently consists of 55 aircraft of four different variants as follows: 46 Series 10, one -10CF, and four each of the -30 and -30CF versions. The Series 10s are used on domestic flights whilst the -30 versions are used on transpacific flights to Hong Kong. For this service some Canadian Pacific aircraft were used in a swap deal in which some Series 10s joined the Canadian airline.

A Canadian Series 30 in full United livery is pictured on final approach to Kai Tak's runway 13. *Robbie Shaw*

Below right:
Turk Hava Yollari (THY) and McDonnell Douglas were the recipients of considerable adverse publicity when DC-10 TC-JAV crashed on 4 March 1974 soon after take-off from Paris-Orly. All 346 passengers and crew were killed, and the cause was traced to the lock mechanism on the rear cargo hatch door which had not locked properly, causing a massive decompression. The aircraft was one of three Series 10 machines which the airline had acquired just over two years earlier. The remaining two in the fleet were withdrawn in 1986, and subsequently served with charter outfits Bogazici and Turkish Air. Photographed at Heathrow in 1987 is TC-JAU named *Istanbul.* *Robbie Shaw*

France's largest independent carrier, Union de Transports Aeriens (UTA) is a member of the KSSU group. The company uses DC-10-30s and Boeing 747s on its many worldwide international flights, ranging from Africa to Australasia, the USA and Pacific area. One unique feature of the company livery is the green passenger doors on the white fuselage. The airline was a victim of international terrorism when one of its DC-10s was blown up in flight by a bomb whilst en route Abidjan-Paris in September 1989. *Peter Asbridge collection*

Left:
Varig of Brazil is the largest airline in South America, and ordered its first DC-10-30s in 1972. When delivered in 1974 these aircraft were in a two/four/two passenger configuration in economy class, but soon afterwards they were changed to the traditional two/five/two the aircraft was designed for. The airline now has a fleet of 12 DC-10-30s, two of which (PP-VMT and PP-VMU) are now in all-cargo -30F configuration. They are used on internal as well as international routes. Flights to Europe are increasingly being flown by Boeing 747s, but DC10s can still be seen at Barcelona, Lisbon, Madrid, Oporto, Paris and Zürich. PP-VMZ is pictured at Rio de Janeiro. *Leo Marriott*

Above:
Venezuela's national carrier, Viasa, took delivery of its first DC-10 in 1978, and immediately commenced operations to the American destinations of Miami and New York, With assistance from KLM, with which it had strong links, the airline expanded its fleet to five of the Series 30 wide-bodies which displaced DC-8s on routes to its many European destinations. The distinctive orange-painted fin stands out against the blue sky as Viasa's DC-10, YV-137C, departs Toronto.
Robbie Shaw

Left:
The name Western Airlines disappeared on 1 April 1987 when it was taken over by Delta Airlines, making the latter one of the largest airlines in the USA. Western was one of America's oldest airlines and operated DC-10-10s on internal services, including Hawaii. A Gatwick to Honolulu service was operated by a Series 10 aircraft via Anchorage; however, load factors were very poor and, of course, the shorter range Series 10 was far from ideal for the route. A longer range Series 30 was leased in 1981 for a Gatwick-Denver service, but again proved unprofitable and the service was discontinued.

Honolulu was one of the profitable destinations in the Western network, which is where DC-10-10 N914WA was photographed landing.
Robbie Shaw

Right:
Maxwell W. Ward started his first company Polaris Charter back in 1946 with a single DH Fox Moth and the name changed to Wardair in 1953. The company has built up dramatically from a charter operator through to the international airline it is today. Three DC-10-30s complemented the fleet of Boeing 747s, and were frequently seen at Gatwick, Prestwick and Ringway, until their disposal in 1988. Seen landing at Toronto is C-GXRC named *Wop May*. The building in the background is McDonnell Douglas Canada where the wings of the DC-10 were made. *Duncan MacIntosh*

Below right:
World Airways has been a successful charter company since its formation in 1948. Scheduled low fare trunk services began in 1979, and the following year international routes were opened to Frankfurt and Gatwick. These services were terminated in 1986 when the company had 11 DC-10s on strength and the airline now concentrates exclusively on charters, including flights on behalf of the US Department of Defense. The current fleet consists of six Series 30CF variants and one of these, N108WA, is seen on approach to Kai Tak. *Robbie Shaw*

A youngster in the aviation world, Zambia Airways was formed as recently as 1967. Flagship of the fleet is the DC-10-30 which joined the company in 1984. From its Lusaka base the type is used on intercontinental routes to Bombay, Frankfurt, Heathrow, New York and Rome. Photographed seconds from touchdown on runway 27L at Heathrow is DC-10-30 N3016Z, named *Nkwazi*. *Robbie Shaw*

Right:

The operator of the largest DC-10 fleet is the United States Air Force's Strategic Air Command, which has 59 KC-10A Extenders in service out of the 60 delivered (one aircraft was lost in 1987). The KC-10A first flew in July 1980, with deliveries commencing the following year to Barksdale Air Force (AFB), La, home of the 2nd Bombardment Wing (BW). The Wing's 32nd Air Refuelling Squadron (ARS) began operations with the type soon afterwards, including support of an Air National Guard A-7 Corsair deployment to Europe, and participation in the Paris Air Show. The Air Force Reserve (AFRES) provides a squadron of personnel to each KC-10 unit and the 78th ARS (Associate) is assigned to the 2nd BW. The associate squadron members spend two weeks on active duty each year, as well as a designated number of weekends. The first 20 or so aircraft delivered were in airliner-type colour scheme, with white upper surfaces, grey undersides, a thin blue cheat-line and blue nose. Subsequent deliveries were in the low-visibility drab grey. The second KC-10 built, 90434, is photographed on the point of touchdown at RAF Wittering at the end of its first deployment to Europe. *Robbie Shaw*

Extenders deploy frequently to the European theatre, where they refuel some NATO aircraft, such as the three Luftwaffe F-4F Phantoms seen with this Barksdale-based KC-10A.
Diethard Achterberg

Left:
**The third and final KC-10 unit is
the 68th ARW at Seymour-
Johnson AFB, NC. It comprises
the 344th and 911th ARS, along
with its AFRES associate unit,
the 77th ARS. Aircraft from the
68th can be identified by the
silhouette of a Wright biplane on
the fin.
Nose art has recently been
re-introduced in Strategic Air
Command units, including
tanker squadrons. An example is
Metal Maiden on KC-10A
600028 of the 68th ARW – note
the toned-down unit badges
near the crew entrance door.**
Robbie Shaw

Overleaf:
**Flightdeck: the second pilot's
seat and instrument display of a
British Airways DC-10.**
Robbie Shaw